KT-529-177

☞ CONTENTS

Off we go!		*4*
1	Lights Out (The Historical Bit)	*5*
2	Saxon Times	*17*
3	Saxon Law and Order	*22*
4	Art Attack	*28*
5	King Arthur (for Real)	*31*
6	King Arthur (the Legend)	*36*
7	Here Come the Vikings!	*52*
8	The End (and The Beginning)	*62*
Time's Up		*64*

☁ OFF WE GO!

Historically speaking, there seems to be a bit of a problem about the difference between two terms: 'Middle Ages' and 'Dark Ages'. It would be nice to report that the Dark Ages started after breakfast, at 9.15am, on the morning of the 21st of February (a Thursday) in AD 410, but I'm afraid that history doesn't work like that. Actually, the Dark Ages were the early bit of what we call the Middle Ages which were so called because (yes, you guessed it) they were in the middle – and they went on for ages. *They* ended in about 1500. What *I'm* calling the Dark Ages ended in 1066 (Norman Conquest). If you wanted to be really picky, you could refer to them as the *Early* Middle Ages, but I think that's boring and anyway who cares. Dark Ages sounds much better and I've already written a book called the Middle Ages – so we'll stick to Dark. OK?*

PS If you see lots of rather annoying comments (like the one below) by someone calling themselves 'Ed.' please just ignore them. It's Susie, my editor, who obviously hasn't got anything better to do.

*I think we get the picture. Ed

Chapter 1

LIGHTS OUT
(THE HISTORICAL BIT)

Where was I? Ah yes – the Dark Ages. It's fair to say that the world went sort of dark* when the Romans, who'd been occupying us for nigh on three centuries, got rather too big for their sandals, lost the plot, declined and then fell. For the next six centuries (the period separating the Ancient and Modern worlds) most countries, and Britain in particular, went into mothballs in terms of culture and development, probably because the people who took the Romans' place were more or less barbarians (please don't ask where Barbaria is).

Meanwhile . . .
The eastern bit of the Roman Empire became the Byzantine Empire (Byzantium became Constantinople which became Istanbul – in Turkey), but much of this was sucked into the mighty

*Metaphorically speaking. Ed
What? JF

Islamic Empire which came along later. The Chinese never got involved in all this conquering nonsense and carried on regardless, forging ahead of the rest of the world in almost everything, including such massive developments as the umbrella and sweet and sour chop suey. As for America, they had always been a bit behind, but by this time huge civilizations and empires were beginning to form that would later turn into household names like Incas and Aztecs. But enough of this foreign stuff – back to Britain and the exciting lead-up to the departure of the Romans.

The Beginning of the End

It all started to go wrong for the Romans in Britain with an East Anglian (Norwich-ian, to be precise) queen called Boudicca.

Useless Fact No. 590

Most people tend to call her Boadicea, but I have it on good authority that this version of her name came from a spelling mistake in a Renaissance manuscript. Some mistake!

London Away-Day

Boudicca, somewhat miffed at the tragic death of her hubby who'd been cheated by the Romans, the rape of her daughters and the flogging of herself (also by the Romans), decided to get the old chariot out in AD 61 and race down to their Londinium headquarters with all her soldiers, to teach the Romans a lesson. She and her hubby had been revolting for a while, because the Romans, in an effort to tame the natives, had tried to take all their lovely weapons away. The revolt had gone on until the Romans got fed up and decided to nip this revolution in the bud. That's why Boudicca (which means 'victory') decided to attack. The old girl must have been a terrifying spectacle with her bottom-length red hair, huge spear and rather cross expression, tearing down the A11* leading a fantastically fierce army in her self-drive, one-woman chariot.

She did OK at first, destroying all the Roman towns on the way south and massacring 70,000 colonists and countless Brits before burning London to the ground (what a lark). Gradually, however, Suetonius, the last great Roman general (Emperor Nero was in charge back home), having got over the shock of being trashed by a mere woman (and a redhead at that), began to get the upper hand, despite being severely outnumbered. Boudicca rather sportingly (please discuss) poisoned herself, thus joining the 80,000 of her army who'd already perished

*I think you'll find the A11 wasn't actually there yet. Ed

(and presumably saving Suetonius the trouble of killing her himself). Her body was never found . . .

Useless Fact No. 593

Loads of severed skulls found underneath what is now Gracechurch Street in the City of London are thought to be the remains of the Roman residents who got in her way.

Romans Go Home

As you might have guessed, the Brits didn't suddenly wake up one morning and notice all the Romans not there. Over the years, the Romans had been gradually sending all their lads back, on account of their own capital, Rome, being attacked on a daily basis. Those poor old Romans! Everywhere they looked were loads of different sorts of barbarians all trying to grab their hard-won empire off 'em.

And it hadn't been just Boudicca and her Iceni army that had been giving the Romans a hard time in Britain. There'd been constant raids from those pesky Scots, Picts and Celts from the North, not to mention the regular arrivals of Saxons in the South. Crikey, I expect they began to think the whole darned place wasn't worth the grief. To make matters worse, there was lots of in-fighting between all the British tribes, many employing tough barbarian mercenaries from abroad to help fight their battles. It was a really rotten period to live in if you were just trying to keep your head down and get on with life. Whole communities were constantly on the move, trying to get out of the way of all the invaders, whose journeys around the country were made much easier, of course, by all those nice straight roads so kindly donated by the recently-departed Romans.

Long Division

Britain, therefore, was pretty much up for grabs and anyone who was anyone was trying to get in on the act – including, as it turned out, a certain King Arthur (we'll get to him soon) who was determined to kick out the foreigners and make us all Christian.

There were four main domains: England, Scotland, Wales and Cornwall. (Ireland, at that time, was completely separate and keeping itself to itself, being, as far as I can make out, almost entirely populated by monks.) Before very long (a couple of hundred years or so) everyone forgot how to talk Latin, how to cook pasta and how to drive Fiats – the Romans were becoming just a distant memory, a nostalgic whiff of garlic on the medieval English breeze.*

*What are you talking about? Ed

England Does the Splits

By the 6th century AD, England had settled down to skirmishing amongst itself. It was like today's football teams, with each one hitting the top of the power league at different times.

Three major kingdoms had now emerged: Mercia in the middle, Northumbria above it and Wessex in the deep south. By now, thanks to an assorted bunch of touring Roman monks headed by a chappie called Saint Augustine – actually, it was Mr Augustine at that time; he was made a saint later – anyway, thanks to these monks, who'd been sent by Pope Gregory the Great, England had become practically all Christian. (Apparently Gregory had seen a bunch of English lads in Rome and commented that they looked more like Angels than Angles, and that's what started it all off.)

Unfortunately, there were all sorts of different Christians and the back-biting and in-fighting started up again. In 664, all the heads of the church got together to try and iron out one version of the truth (like getting politicians to agree about what day of the week it is). They eventually decided on the Roman version at something called a Synod (a religious conference) at somewhere called Whitby.

Musical Chairs

The next few centuries were confusing to say the least.

Much of the 7th was ruled by Northumbria under King Edwin, who chipped away at his southern border taking more and more out of Mercia. Edinburgh was his capital city.

Then, in the 8th century, the mysterious and extraordinary King Offa (special Offa – geddit?) of Mercia took over, driving the wilful Welsh behind a great dyke (yes! Offa's Dyke) that he'd built specially for the job.*

By the time the 9th century came along, it was Wessex's turn and they went one better, taking over the whole of England with a brand new king, the jolly good Egbert (see Silly Names for Ancient Kings). Egbert's kingdom was a bit odd: primitive farms and villages separated by acres of wasteland,

*I doubt he built it himself. Ed.

and deserted towns and cities with their inhabitants practically camping out between the eerie ruins of magnificent deserted Roman buildings.

Good as he was, poor old King Egbert, being without a proper government, couldn't handle such a big domain. He relied on loyal citizens to supply an army, but there wasn't a proper warrior among them: most of the natives had forgotten how to fight . . . They were like sitting ducks for the hordes of stroppy would-be illegal immigrants who'd been lining up to pounce on what was regarded as a very precious prize – Britain!

Vikings Ahoy!

If you want to know all about the Vikings and their invasions, for it was them that were a-knocking at the door, you'll have to shell out another couple of quid and buy my book called . . . um . . . *Vikings*.

Just to sum up, however, those horribly horny (on their hats) men began with a few sneaky pillages (of the villages) in the 8th century and by the 9th were at it continually. It had become a full-scale invasion.

Alfred Ahoy!

They were finally pulled up by the great Alfred (the Great) who was currently king of Wessex. A bit later he also deterred the Danes who were coming the other way and made sure that they turned round and went back to be nice Normans in Normandy, France. Nice, that is, until they came back and conquered us in 1066 . . . but that's another book (*Middle Ages*, a gift at £1.99).*

*That's enough advertising. Ed

Europe Ahoy!

All the countries which had fallen under the spell of the Christian church now turned into 'Europe' and were operating under the feudal system, but Britain was slowly cutting herself off from the rest of the world. The big question seems to be: what *really* happened when the Romans scurried back to Rome in AD 410? What was Britain like? Well, according to the Confessions of St Patrick, patron saint of the Irish, things carried on much the same as before for a good few years after they'd gone. They had the same sort of government and the same sort of control by the rich (who'd learned all the Romans' bad habits) over the poor (who, bless 'em, did as they were told).

Saxons Ahoy!

Without the Roman soldiers there to protect it, English society was a trifle vulnerable and it wasn't long before their warlike enemies glimpsed an opportunity. The English had been urgently calling (reverse charge) their Roman ex-masters to ask if they could possibly send any help against the awful Picts and Scots who were giving it plenty up on the northern borders (if you call jumping over Hadrian's Wall 'plenty'!). When no one answered, Angle and Saxon mercenaries from Germany and Denmark were brought in by a certain English leader called Vortigern (sounds like a loo cleaner) to help. And that's where all the trouble started.

England, under an all-powerful leader, became quite settled and prosperous, and was now well able to keep out the ghastly northerners, but the thousands of Anglo-Saxon mercenaries were getting restless and, led by a chap called Hengist and his mate Horsa, revolted in the late 440s.

Meanwhile, just to keep the Brits on their feet, there were another lot of German tribes raiding our coastline and spreading haddock wherever they landed.*

Britain Declines

Britain's wonderful Roman cities, our pride and joy, were literally falling apart. The warlike and severely downmarket Anglo-Saxons were not turned on by art or beauty and were only really interested in keeping invaders out. (Can you blame them?) Consequently many cities fell into total desolation and some were even abandoned if the residents thought they couldn't be properly defended. Many new towns, therefore, grew up round castles or big manor houses. Some warlords even went back to do up the old, abandoned hill forts which

*Shouldn't that be havoc? Ed

they'd had to leave when the Romans first pitched up. Instead of all the nice civilized Christian- and Roman-influenced English people being threatened by the horrid, rough Celts, it was the other way round. The English were now a bunch of savages threatening the recently Christianized Celts. These new Christians in Britain needed a hero and the guy they chose was a chap called Arthur (see Chapters 5 and 6).

Kings-a-plenty

Everyone was going King-Krazy in those days and before long England had *seven* of 'em, each with a dinky little kingdom of his very own. These were (if I remember rightly) Kent, Sussex, Essex, Wessex (south), Northumbria, East Anglia and Mercia (Midlands). Blimey, just think of all that blue blood swilling around the country . . . some people think we have enough trouble these days supporting one lot!

There then followed a couple of extremely boring centuries where hardly anyone had anything to fight about, so got on with farming and increasing the population.

Viking Alert

But reports were coming in about strange, blond, bearded men, of an extremely fierce disposition, wearing funny clothes and pointy hats with horns on, attacking the north of England and raping and pillaging all who came in their path . . . It was the dreaded Vikings from Denmark and these occasional seaside raids soon turned into a full invasion. They were stopped by our Alfred the Great, who held a lot of them at bay while the rest shot over to France and turned into Normans.*

*This all sounds horribly simplistic. Ed
I told you I was in a hurry. JF

All went well until King Ethelred the Unready decided to kill all the Danes that had stayed behind – which really annoyed their Viking brothers when news got back home. Sven Forkbeard, the Danish king (whose sister, by the way, had been one of those who were massacred), came over and, after a lot of toing and froing, captured England.

This particular Scandinavian Empire didn't last that long, and Ethelred's son, Edward the Confessor, soon got England back again (this is a bit like international snakes and ladders). Soon afterwards, however, in 1066, the Normans threw double-sixes and shot up the lader, conquering England and heralding the end of the Dark Ages.

Chapter 2

SAXON TIMES

When the Saxon invaders realized that the Romans weren't coming back, all that conquering and hell-raising became rather tedious. I mean, you can't just burn and plunder for ever – there'd be nothing left to steal – and anyway, they had it all. Much more to the point, sooner or later someone would have to grow crops and rear animals and all that boring malarkey, if they were going to eat. Those Saxons who didn't bring their own women with them (that is, the Saxons who didn't have any women to bring) soon got round the female residents and instead of ravishing them and sending them home to be slaves, married 'em instead, and settled down.

EARLY
MAD
COWS
↓

Useless Fact No. 599

The Britons simply referred to the invaders as Saxons, but there were many tribes involved, including the Angles, the Jutes and the Frisians (large black and white cows?).*

*Don't be ridiculous. Ed

After Arthur

A hundred years after the semi-legendary Arthur's semi-legendary death in AD 520, the Saxons were on the move again, completely destroying the now leaderless Britons' resistance. The poor things were driven far into the mountains of the West and North where they lived rather unhappily ever after . . .

Pleasant Peasants

Saxon peasants or *ceorls* chose to work under the protection of a lord or *thane* who lived up at the big 'ouse, rather than trying to go it alone in the 'ard, dark world. There were three brands of peasant.

At the top were the *geneatus* who paid rent and gave the lord a pig each year to secure pasture rights. They were expected to reap the boss's 'arvest and show visitors to the manor 'ouse.

Lower down was the *cottar* or *bordar*, who was excused rent but 'ad to do a whole load of duties every Monday (and every day in August). It wasn't the best deal in the 'ole* wide world. For reaping an acre of his master's corn he'd only receive a sheaf (large bunch) of corn in payment.

Below him was the *gebur* or *villein*. He was given about thirty acres of land, but for that he had to work at least two days a week for his lord.

YOU KNOW WHAT YOU CAN DO WITH THAT!

*Stop it. Ed

On top of that he'd be expected to do other work, like plough a couple of acres of his master's land a year as rent and act as guardian of his master's sheep. On top of *that* he had to pay the old man two pence a year, a couple of chickens at Christmas and twenty odd bushels of barley. That was when he was alive. When he died, the master could step in and grab all his possessions, making his family into beggars.

Serf Alert
Right at the bottom was the *serf* (or slave) who everyone looked down on. A man was usually born a serf, but some freemen who lost all their money would sell themselves and their family into serfdom, which basically meant that they became slaves of the master in return for food and shelter.

Peasant-wear
Peasant men continued to wear the sort of thing that they'd been wearing for donkey's years: very itchy, woollen tunics with wooden clogs or crude leather shoes. The women wore long tunics covering all of their bodies and a veil with a hole for the face. Not very interesting, really.

Rich-wear
Men favoured loose-fitting trousers, belted and fastened with those criss-cross garters of leather and cloth that you see in all the pictures. Over this would be a loose tunic and a cloak fastened at the shoulders.

Rich women dressed a bit like Maid Marion – Robin Hood's girlfriend (even though she wasn't to come along for a few hundred years – in those days fashion didn't change every time some silly designer in Paris sneezed, as it does now). Over a long, light-coloured undergown with tight sleeves, your Dark Ages posh-person would wear a three-quarter length, heavily embroidered overgown (or *roc* – from which we get 'frock') with large, full sleeves; on top of all that she'd wear a large embroidered cloak that trailed along the ground after her – unless some lesser mortal was good enough to carry it. Unlike the itchy poor people she'd wear nice smooth cotton underwear. Women would also wear tons of heavy but cleverly worked hippy-ish metal jewellery. Their hair would be braided, coiled at the back, and then hidden by some sort of head-dress.

Hair Today

Hair was worn long and a bit hippy-ish, but beards and moustaches were regarded as a bit downmarket – especially on the women.

Saxon Fun

Before we go any further, it must be said that it was only the wealthy that had any real fun. The poor just worked and then slept, going to bed when it got dark as they didn't have candles. If the peasants wanted any relief they'd have physical competitions or go to church and to celebrate festivals. (Yippee!)

Food for the Rich

The rich folk got through mountains of food – mostly meat and cereals (not much call for veg) all washed down with copious booze (ale and mead) which they drank from horns (goblets weren't used much). Since they couldn't stand up on their own (the horns) the drinkers tended to drink their drinks all in one go, which usually led to them (the drinkers) not being able to stand up on their own either.*

There was quite a lot of competition amongst the aristocratic thane class as to who could give the best social events, and they'd give splendid gifts to their guests to try and outdo each other. After a big meal, the women would leave and all the guys would sit around listening to music played on the harp or primitive pipes, boasting about their bravery in various bygone battles. This often led to new ones!

Useless Fact No. 603

If you were a cow, a sheep or a pig it was a good idea to lie low around November. This was known as 'Blot monath', meaning the 'blood month', when all unnecessary animals were murdered by their masters, who couldn't afford to keep them through the long, cold winters.

*Eh? Ed

Chapter 3

SAXON LAW AND ORDER

Dealing with crime in the Dark Ages was a bit similar to the Wild West of America a hundred years ago. As there was no police force, Dark Ages criminals had to be hunted down with a posse (bunch of ordinary people who've been pulled in to help the sheriff*) and then dealt with on the spot. For smaller offences, a suspect would be tracked down by his 'tithing'. A tithing was a group of twelve men to which each male over twelve had to belong. They were collectively responsible for each other's good behaviour. There was no official imprisonment, since keeping someone in jail cost money (it still does!). It was far easier to kill or banish them (some say it still would be!). That's not to say that some poor souls didn't get thrown into castle dungeons, but meal times were usually forgotten – even elevenses – so they didn't last too long.

EARLY OPTIMISM

A LITTLE MORE SUGAR PLEASE!

*They didn't have sheriffs in the Dark Ages. Ed

Kindred

If someone was killed it was their family or *kindred* who prosecuted the offender and who collected the *wergild*, two thirds of which went to their dad's family and a third of which to their mum's. If it was only a serf that was murdered, his master would cop the loot. Sometimes this money would be refused if the family preferred a gang war with the other man's family. People's kindred also arranged marriages and acted as insurance should a member of the family be poorly and not able to work.

How Much are you Worth?

Every freeman had a money value in Saxon times, so if an innocent man was unfortunate enough to get murdered, the murderer and/or his family would be expected to shell out a set amount, on top of anything else (execution, etc.) that might happen. Killing a 'thane' (upper-class person), was quite an expensive business – at least 6000 silver pennies – while the lower classes weighed in at about 1000, unless, of course, you were the lowest of the low, i.e. of British descent, in which case it would be half that (what a cheek). If a freeman was merely injured, like having a broken leg or a stab wound, he could expect about 50 silver pennies from the guy that did it. The worst thing to do would be to kill one of the royal bodyguard (or king's thane): that would cost a cool 12 grand.

Worst of the Worst

The baddest thing you could possibly do was to be disloyal or treacherous to the king. That would not only be instant death, but all your worldly goods would be confiscated. Any form of murder or robbery in public (it was far better to do it at home), or setting fire to other people's property, also carried the death sentence.

Hide and Seek

Hiding in England was quite easy in those days, as it was mostly forest. But hiding wasn't all jolly Robin Hood-type fun, as being outlawed in those early days was often a long, slow death sentence. If the cold and damp and wolves (or squirrels) didn't get you, you were liable to be killed on sight if you set foot outside the woods. Anyone could kill an outlaw just for the fun of it.

Useless Fact No. 605

For saying nasty things, or for simply telling porkies, it was quite common to have your tongue cut out, and if you were caught passing or making fake money, your hand would be cut off and nailed to a door. Charming.

Trial Time

Most crimes were, of course, denied and since there were no police or detectives to investigate further, trials were rather hit and miss affairs. Decisions were either up to the public, or the village elders, at assemblies called 'footmoots' or 'shiremoots' which later developed into courts (or 'courtmoots'?).

Worst of all were the dreaded 'trials by ordeal'. If the plaintiff failed to appear, he was guilty – no further questions asked. If he or his family couldn't afford the fine, he became an outlaw and was banished. It was usually helpful to have witnesses, but this was all a bit daft because the suspect's family would be *expected* to swear on oath that he or she was innocent. If the accuser's oath was accepted, a Trial by Ordeal would follow. At first the defendant was urged to confess, then, after a long, slow fast, he was allowed to take the Holy Sacrament, effectively begging God to see him through the ordeal. This is where it gets nasty . . .

Sink or Swim . . . A popular test of the time was by water. The accused was made to drink holy water (punishment enough, I'd have thought), and was then bound and gagged, and chucked into a river or lake or stream or sea or puddle or bucket or—* If he floated, he was guilty, but if he sank, he was innocent (drowned and dead usually – but innocent).

Carrying the Weight . . . Alternatively, he might be asked nicely to carry a red-hot metal weight for three paces. If he dropped it he was in big trouble.

*That's enough, thank you. Ed

Hand-Dipping . . . Sometimes the trial would require the accused to dunk his hand in boiling water and retrieve a stone. After the last two kinds of trial, the hand(s) would be bound, but if, after three days, the wounds were still blistered or had festered, he'd automatically be found guilty.

Useless Fact No. 607

Some societies in North Africa and the Middle East apparently still do stuff like this. It's common for Bedouins to place a red-hot spoon on the tongue of the accused to see if it burns.

Join the Clubs

Another way of settling a dispute was for the plaintiff and the accused to fight it out with heavy wooden clubs. The one that gave in yelled 'craven' and lost his case. I think they should try that again today. Not exactly fair – but jolly effective.

Anyone for Magic

Everyone in the olden days believed in fairies, witches and things that go *bump* in the night. Magic spells and charms were all the rage. When a cow was stolen (a regular event) the ex-owner would cast a spell against the thief. It might go something like this:

> *'Bethlehem was called the town wherein Christ was born:*
> *it is famed over the earth.*
> *So may this deed be in the sight of men.'*

Then he'd say a bit of Latin and then turn to the east and yell three times:

'May the cross of Christ bring it back from the East.'

He'd repeat this in each direction, and finish up by chanting:

'So may this deed never be concealed!'

It didn't bring the cow back but usually made him feel better.

Sick as a Beetle

These charms and sayings were used against illness too, which was just as well as doctors and surgeons hadn't been invented. If someone had a tummy-ache, they'd search the ground until they found a dung beetle digging in the earth. They'd then have to scoop up the beetle and eat it . . .

No they didn't – I lied. They'd have to wave the beetle to and fro saying *'Cure my belly-ache!'* (in Latin) and then throw the beetle over their shoulder. Seems a bit unfair on the beetle.

Chapter 4

ART ATTACK

When the Romans left our shores, art and culture went with 'em. The constant battles that followed left hardly any time to study the finer things of life, and soon all that wonderful drawing, sculpture and architecture was well forgotten.

Christianity was also partly to blame because, as it spread through the country, the only art produced was by the church. And that's where it all went wrong. Most of the early religious leaders frowned on anything that looked remotely like fun. Worshipping God was a dead serious business, not to be taken lightly. There must have been some artists in the churches and monasteries who looked back wistfully to a time when people knew how to draw and sculpt properly but, let's face it, when you have angry Angles, Jutes, Saxons and Vikings knocking down your door every five minutes, your concentration tends to wander a little.

HOW TO MAKE A CELT CROSS

Their 'art', although striking and dynamic, was only there to glorify God in the most direct way possible (and to terrify the wits out of everybody else). Originality was frowned on.* When asking an artist to do some work, most churchmen just wanted something a bit like the bloke in the church down the road had.

When you look at the art of the Dark Ages, it's as if someone had stood over the artists, slapping their wrists if they produced anything even approaching realism. Even so, many of their designs were mystically beautiful and ridiculously intricate and controlled.

Import-art

The various Saxon tribes brought many cunning crafts to Britain, including metalwork and intricate silversmithery, while the Vikings were great at chopping things out of wood and stone (and monks!) . . .

Those Viking craftsmen loved nothing better than getting down to the really intricate stuff and the more they could entwine the bodies of dragons, sea monsters and weird birds, the better. Most of their art was created to bring them luck and to act as charms against the powers of evil, which was quite important if you were in the highly risky invasion business. It has even been said that those carvings of fierce dragon's heads on the fronts of their boats were removed as they sailed into their home ports, in case they frightened the local gods.

The monks of Celtic Ireland and Saxon England rather liked all this complicated Viking stuff and had a bash at ripping it off – sorry – applying it to the Christian religion, especially in their carvings on and in churches. Best of all, however, were

*What do you know about originality? Ed

the fantastic manuscripts like the awe-inspiring Lindisfarne Gospel of AD 700, which features a mass of twirling intertwined serpents and dragony-type things against a black background. Unfortunately, when they came to drawing people, the monks weren't so successful, and usually they looked like they'd drawn by a seven-year old (and that, believe me, is rude to seven-year olds).

Chapter 5

KING ARTHUR
(FOR REAL)

Everyone loves the stories of King Arthur: the Round Table, the Holy Grail, Merlin the magician, the gorgeous (but naughty) Guinevere, Camelot Castle, the Sword in the Lake (and in the Stone) and all the rest of it. Unfortunately, they could well be a bunch of fairy stories, about as believable as the Teletubbies or Star Trek, kept alive by sad people who love the idea of a Golden Age when men were heroes and women did what they were told. Very little was written down in the period between the Romans being shown the red card and the Vikings rushing onto the pitch (our pitch). Such legends are therefore quite difficult to disprove.

Proper historians do, however, firmly believe that there *was* a fabulous leader who fought bravely against the Saxon invaders, but when challenged, they scratch their heads through lack of evidence. This must be a great relief to all Ye Olde Tea and Gifte Shoppes, wacky cults and other strange organizations that try to cash in on the Arthurian legends.

Before we start, we do know for completely sure that the popular image of Arthur and his playmates, in all that fab armour that you see in the storybooks, must have been exaggerated – cos people didn't get tin-wear like that for nearly a thousand years.

Glastonbury

In the Dark Ages there was a huge movement to make Glastonbury Abbey the very cradle of the Christian religion. Instead of using some old saint as front man like other monasteries did, these monks chose a king – a warlord – and wrapped him up in legends of the Holy Grail. This Grail was the cup our Jesus was supposed to have used at the Last Supper. Joseph of Arimathea was also reckoned to have used it to catch Jesus's blood at the crucifixion and brought it to Glastonbury where it seems to have been mislaid – or nicked. The legend had it that only the best and most honest of Arthur's knights would ever be able to come into its presence, provided, that is, that they'd managed to track the darn thing down.

Useless and Unreliable Fact No. 608

In 1181, just after the Abbey had been wrecked by fire, the monks at Glastonbury 'discovered' the remains of a huge man buried in a tree trunk. They said it was yer actual King Arthur and forged an inscription to prove it – just what their restoration fund needed.* Most historians still refer to this spot as the burial place of King Arthur and the original site of Camelot. It must be true cos there's still a plaque there that says so.

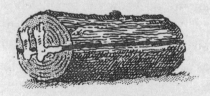

*That's a very cynical attitude, Mr Farman. *Ed*

Useless Fact No. 613

Since then, Arthur's body has been found in loads of places, each with an inscription proving its authenticity and claiming to be the original Camelot. Where there's myth there's money!

The earliest references to our English King Arthur came from two bits of, strangely enough, Welsh writing: *Historia Britonum* and the *Annals of Wales*, which described him as a Welsh hero who led their Chieftains into twelve battles against barbarian invaders.

Four Things Arthur Could have Been

(According to *The Lives of Saints*, a famous Welsh book written in the eleventh century . . .)

1. St Cadoc said Arthur was a quarrelsome leader, who went with loads of wanton wenches and gambled with his mates, Kay and Belvedere, on Welsh hilltops.

2. St Padarn described Arthur as a man who really admired his (Padarn's) tunic and was always trying to get it off him (less said about that the better).

3. St Carantoc reckoned he was a useless dragon-fighter, as he couldn't even defend his fellow countrymen against the

'SCUSE ME YOUNG MAN— ARE YOU LOOKIN FOR SOMEON

local dragon. Also, he accused him of being a petty thief who was forever trying to convert Carantoc's portable altar into an ordinary table.*

4. St Gildasc described Arthur as a strong ruler who'd trashed all the opposition, but whose wife had been stolen by Melwas, King of the Summer Country.

But it was the *History of the Britons*, written in 1130 by Geoffrey de Monmouth, that launched Arthur into superstardom. Before this, none of the Camelot, Merlin, Sword in the Lake stuff had ever been heard of – however, there was just enough history in it to make it believable. The Welsh were naturally a bit hacked off, because Geoff (the author) based their national hero in Cornwall (Tintagel) and not Wales. I doubt whether Mr de Monmouth worried either way, as it became one of the first ever best-sellers. He'd've laughed all the way to the bank (if they'd had any).

*Why? Ed
Search me. JF

. . . at Home

Whoever Arthur was, his job (if you were wondering) was to rouse the Celtic Britons and stop the Saxons taking over the whole of England, as they really wanted to, either by force or infiltration. Some say he led the Cumbrian Cymrys against the invading Saxon pirates as well as the Picts and Scots. Whatever he did, they seem to agree that he certainly delayed those Saxons from taking over Devon and Cornwall for a while.

Arthur led the Britons into twelve battles. At the Battle of Badon (AD 520: Arthur's last battle), 960 of his enemies fell in one single charge (and he killed 'em all). I wonder what the rest of his soldiers were doing?

. . . and Abroad

It is also claimed that Arthur, flushed with success, took a trip abroad and conquered Norway, Denmark and France (before lunch) and then very kindly slew all of Spain's giants before heading off for Rome (quite a trip). The campaign was cut short because reports of Guinevere's exploits (at night with his knights) coming from home were getting a touch embarrassing. He rushed back to Camelot just in time to sort out Lancelot and confront Mordred, his nephew, who was organizing a bit of a rebellion.

Hmm . . .

And this was supposed to be the 'real' bit!

Chapter 6

KING ARTHUR
(THE LEGEND)

Setting the Scene

Once upon a long, long time ago, Britain was half taken over by the very same Saxon mercenaries that King Vortigern had hired from abroad to fight for him (to keep the other Saxons out). When Vortigern burned to death in his half-finished castle (typical British workmanship), the British people flocked to his successor, King Aurelius, and together they defeated all the Saxons and stopped Hengist, their leader, quite effectively – by chopping his head off.

At this time a rather odd lad called Merlin was learning the family business of sorcery and magic, and was given a nice room (if you didn't mind stairs) at the top of one of the palace's lofty towers.

ABRACADABRA – LET THERE BE A LIFT

One day, much later, when King

Aurelius found himself dying, he asked Merlin if he'd build him a really mega monument – one that would last for ages. Cunning old Merlin thought it a bit of a drag to build a new one, but had heard of a collection of huge old stones in Ireland called the Giant's Ring which he thought would do nicely. Without further ado, he and an army of men nicked 'em and brought 'em back to England where they still stand and are called – have you guessed? – Stonehenge!

Useless Fact No. 609

Strangely enough, the boffins reject this theory out of hand. They also reject the theory that the stones were dragged from far away by the Celts. The most popular (and boring) version is that the huge stones were dropped by a passing glacier – during the Ice Age.

New King Time

Next up was good King Uther, who for ten years scoured the country with his army looking for people to fight, either in little wars or in tournaments (he obviously found court life far too boring).

There was this real babe called Igrayne who he fancied like mad since she was by far the best-looking girl in the land. The only snag was that she was already married to a much older guy called Gorlois, Duke of Cornwall and the British Chancellor. Kings generally get what they want, and Uther promptly declared Gorlois a traitor and laid siege to their Cornish love-nest for over a week before Merlin kindly informed him that the dame wasn't even at home; she was at Tintagel castle up the road.

Merlin asked that in return for coming up with a nifty

scheme to get the king into Igrayne's bed that night, they (Uther and Igrayne) must have a baby for him to bring up (Merlin must have wanted a nipper without all the trouble of having one himself – seems fair to me).

The trick worked a doddle. Merlin specialized in disguise and dressed Uther up to look like Igrayne's old man – old white-haired Gorlois. Then he sent Uther off to the impenetrable Tintagel Castle, with a couple of others disguised as Gorlois' men. On arrival, they told the guards that they'd escaped from Uther's siege for the night so that the boss could spend it with his missus (sounds reasonable). This he duly did, or rather, Uther duly did, and, believe it or not, she was none the wiser for having slept with him rather than her hubby (if you believe that, you'll believe anything). Actually, it turned out later that she'd rather fancied Uther all along.*

Well, it really wasn't poor old Gorlois' day. He really *had* tried to slip away to see his wife that night (coincidence or what?), but the enemies outside had spotted and promptly slain him. Just as well, or poor Igrayne would have had two Gorloises to sleep with. The *real* one and the Uther.

*This is like the *News of the World*. Ed.

Arthur's Arrival

No prizes for guessing the name of the child born exactly nine months later. Young Arthur was given to Merlin, as promised, and he in turn handed the baby over to a couple to do all the messy stuff, as they already had a five-year-old son called Kay (odd name for a boy). Uther was well pleased as he not only got to marry Igrayne, but he also didn't have all those nappies to change.

Arthur was no ordinary lad and grew up to be the strongest, fastest, bravest, handsomest, cleverest (in fact, every 'est' going) boy in the land. But, like all good legends, there was a bit of a snag. Arthur's mum had a couple of daughters from her first marriage with old (now dead) Gorlois. When Igrayne married Uther, one of them, Morgan le Fay, just loathed her new dad and the unborn child from the start – cursing them both big time. It must have been a slow-acting curse, as nothing happened for a couple of years until, out of the blue, Uther keeled over, for no apparent reason (that's curses for you).

New King Time Again

After Uther died, Igrayne ruled, but was pretty useless at it and soon the whole country was fighting again. Merlin told her tactfully that she was a terrible queen and so she and her ministers agreed to crown a new king at Westminster. Every duke, earl and knight in the country was told to attend (or else), and London soon became chock-a-block with nobility.

All very well, but . . . There was the old archbish, waiting, crown in hand, ready for action, but they hadn't decided who was going to wear it. After a big service, in which they all prayed for guidance, the congregation walked out of the

Cathedral to find, practically blocking the doorway, a huge lump of marble with a steel anvil set into it and a beautiful sword set into that. (How did it get there? Who put it there? Nobody seems to ask tricky questions in legends.) An inscription on the stone read:

'*Whoever can draw the sword is the rightful king of all Britain.*' Everyone ran off for their sketchpads hoping to do the best drawing. No they didn't, that's a joke.* But seriously, all the lords pulled for ages but the blinking sword wouldn't budge.

Tournament Time

In the end they got bored with trying and rushed off to have a tournament, forgetting all about the sword. Kay, Arthur's foster brother, was now grown up and one of the competitors, but he'd forgotten his sword (silly ass) so he sent 16-year-old Arthur back to their lodgings to get it. Unfortunately, the house was locked up, but on the way back Arthur noticed this old sword sticking out of the stone outside the cathedral and reckoned he'd . . . er, 'borrow' it.

He promptly pulled it out and took it to Kay. Everyone recognized the sword in Kay's hand, and Kay, being no fool (and a liar), said it was his and that he must be king. But Kay's dad had seen what had happened and told him off, telling

*And what a joke it was. Ed.

.

Arthur (his foster son) to show everyone how he'd done it. A puzzled Arthur (who still didn't know about his own background) did it over and over again (show-off), which got up the noses of the other lords and knights no end. They argued for hours that it was just one of Merlin's stunts (which, let's face it, it probably was).

Then they all noticed how much the boy looked like his dead dad, good King Uther, and fell on their knees yelling 'Long Live King Arthur!' About time too.

War Time

At first things went well – but then rumours started drifting in that all the second division kings round England were getting too big for their chainmail and were planning a rebellion. Arthur was told that there was an army of 100,000 gathering. Poor Arthur only had 10,000 blokes handy, so it was a bit of a poser. Merlin, bless him, once again saved the day by dashing off to France (Eurostar? Non!) to talk to a few of England's allies. 20,000 French soldiers set off right away, but Arthur's mob were still hopelessly outnumbered, as your sums should tell you. However, the heavily-armed smaller army jumped the bigger rebel army while they were asleep (still in their jim-jams) and so won a famous battle at Mons Badonicus. The naughty kings were made to stand in the corner and forced to promise to be good in future.

Love Time

It was about this time that Arthur met Guinevere, a dead tasty and rather posh bird, and fell hopelessly in love with her. Before anything happened (nudge, nudge), news came in from

France that a giant called a 'warlow' had murdered and eaten thousands of poor French folk and had carried off the Duke and Duchess of Brittany to his lair on the island of Mont St Michel. Now, as you will remember, Arthur owed the French a big favour, so Merlin and Arthur set out with a few chosen men, including his brother (now *Sir* Kay), across the channel that night. When they got there everyone was hiding from the 'warlow' so it was all a bit spooky.

They finally arrived at the island but it turned out that the duchess had already copped it, and the duke was still chained up in the dungeons. Arthur soon came upon the giant, licking his lips while his poor servant-girls were roasting four young children on spits over the fire (a light snack before bedtime, no doubt). The giant leapt up, club in hand, but Arthur sliced his ankle off, which made him fall over. Arthur then cut off the giant's head for good measure (unfortunately it was too late for the kids, as they were, by this time, done to a turn). Arthur returned to England a massive hero and everyone thought he was fab.

HOW LONG DO CHILDREN TAKE?

EARLY BBQ

Tricky Times Ahead
Oh dear, oh dear. Poor Arthur had it bad for Guinevere and they were to be married. Remember Morgan, the half-sister

that had cursed him before he was even born? Well, she still had it in for him, and drugged him before sending her sister, Morgause, who'd always fancied her half-brother, into Arthur's bedroom while he was asleep. In his dozy state, Arthur thought it was Guinevere and you can guess what happened. Morgause got pregnant and it was left to poor old Merlin to break the news to Arthur.

Excalibur

Merlin was getting on a bit, but before retiring, he wanted to give Arthur a new sword (who'd managed to break the one that all the fuss was about). Now, old Merlin couldn't do anything in a normal way and so one day took Arthur to the side of a lake and told him he'd located a magic sword. They slept by the lake that night and by the morning Arthur was beginning to wonder when and where and *if* the new sword was ever going to turn up.

Just then, Arthur noticed this hand coming out of the lake holding what looked like a rather nice weapon. He and Merlin got into a little boat (there's always one at hand in legends, isn't there?) and rowed out to get it. The hand turned out to be joined to an arm which turned out be joined to a submerged, black-haired woman who turned out to be the 'Lady of the Lake' (who turned out to be one of Merlin's old chums). The sword, Excalibur, was not only magic, but unbreakable and able to cut through metal. But there was just one hitch: it couldn't be touched by anyone but Arthur, and it had to be returned to the lake when he'd finished with it.

Mission accomplished, Merlin then retired to a cave and practised tricks and potions for the rest of his life.

The Round Table

Mr and Mrs Arthur had got their fab castle Camelot just the way they liked it. Luckily Guinevere had come with a whole load of good quality furniture, amongst which was this massive round table and a load of chairs that had once belonged to King Uther, who'd given it to her dad. She'd secretly wanted it as a dining-room table but Arthur had other ideas. He'd been looking for something to sit round with all his knights (150 of them!) to discuss things like who they were going to fight next. To get a place round that table meant you'd really arrived in the knights' super-league.

After the marriage, they had a fantastic tournament where all the best fighters came from far and wide. But one mysterious guy beat absolutely everyone. He turned out to be called Lancelot, and when he took his helmet off, the new Queen Guinevere fancied him instantly (not too good a sign when you've only just got married). Anyway, Lancelot joined the Round Table, was knighted and became Arthur's best mate and top knight. But trouble loomed, as you might have guessed.

HELLO THERE!

From day one Lancelot became Guinevere's champion. He always wore her colours and fought just for her, which would have started me thinking all sorts of things if I had been her husband.

Hunt the Grail

One day an old tramp pitched up at the castle mumbling about the Fisher King and the Holy Grail (whatever they were), and about a bloke who was going to turn up looking for this Grail thing, and who would break the whole comfy Camelot scenario apart. As soon as he'd said it, he died, and Lancelot – for reasons best known to himself – set off to find this Fisher King guy. Just before he left, however, Guinevere took him to one side and made a big pass at him. Read on . . .

What's Cooking?

Lancelot had only been away a couple of days before he stumbled across this tower from which came the sounds of a girl screaming. It appeared that the girl had insulted the evil Morgan le Fay (remember?) and she was being boiled alive, to teach her a lesson. Lancelot broke into the tower and, battling through the steam, rescued the lobster-like girl and

took her outside. The tower, by the way, instantly collapsed in dust behind him. Just for good measure, Lancelot killed a dragon who'd been annoying the locals (setting fire to things, eating people and so on).

The Fisher King

To cut an extremely long story extremely short, Lancelot eventually found the Fisher King (one of a long line of kings in charge of the Holy Grail). The present one (King Pelleam) was in a real state, and his castle and lands were in ruins. Everything had gone wrong following a terrible stab wound that was still bleeding after many years. They'd been waiting for a brave knight to come and heal it (I'd have thought a doctor might have been more use), and take charge of the poor old Grail, a fabulous golden cup, which had been kicking around gathering dust.

After a first-class meal the night he'd arrived, Lancelot lay in bed dreaming of – yup – Guinevere. Suddenly he woke up and there was this naked girl called Elayne (the king's daughter) next to him, claiming that they'd had naughties while he was asleep (some knights have all the luck) and that the baby (that she'd no doubt have) was going to be the one to heal the king *and* take care of the Grail. She then told Lancelot that *he* couldn't do it, cos he had to be perfect and he wasn't – cos he fancied another guy's wife (Arthur's actually).

Home Alone

So poor old Lancelot went home to Camelot, leaving the pregnant princess and the Holy Grail.* Unfortunately, Guinevere had heard on the grapevine about what had happened, and didn't believe a word of his story (can you blame her?), saying she would never speak to him again – bit of a cheek when you consider she was still married to his boss.

Lancelot left Camelot yet again and became a bum, living off leaves and berries. He eventually got thin, mad and really

*Sounds like a good title for a film. Ed

disgusting, until one day, wandering aimlessly in the Fisher King's tragically wrecked wastelands, he bumped into Princess Elayne, who had his son, the perfect Galahad, in the pram. She took old Lance back to the castle, fed him up, and there they lived together for years as husband and wife.

DON'T I KNOW YOU FROM SOMEWHERE?

Late Arrival

One day some visitors arrived from Camelot. Lancelot realized that he still loved dear old Guinevere and felt he must do something about it. Everyone went crazy when he turned up in Camelot, out of the blue, and the party seemed to go on for ever. (What about Elayne and her baby, eh?!)

A little while later, Galahad, now grown-up, also turned up at King Arthur's court and was quickly recognized as perfect knight material. They were all sitting down to supper one night, when a white dove fluttered in, carrying a golden bowl in its beak, with a fragrant vapour issuing from it. A sumptuous meal appeared as if by magic (must have been from the Holy Grail Take-Away) and then the golden bowl spoke (as bowls did in those days), saying: 'I am the Holy Grail and only a perfect knight may come and find me in order to heal the king [who was STILL bleeding], mend the castle and make all the lands good again.'

Of course all the knights (a cocky bunch if ever there was) thought they were pretty near perfect, so next day every last one of 'em left to trail the Grail leaving poor Arthur and Guinevere alone in their massive castle facing each other at breakfast across an empty Round Table.*

No Joy

After a year the knights began to dribble back home, having had no joy in their quest (in fact, half of them had died in the search). One of them was Lancelot (who'd been off being a tramp again) and who had rather daftly confessed to the court how he felt about Arthur's wife, but had promised to be a good boy in future. On his travels, he had found the Holy Grail again at the old, derelict castle but knew that he wasn't the guy destined to bring it back.

Galahad and a couple of chums eventually arrived at his old home, his grandad's castle, and (because he was perfect) Galahad finally cured poor old Pelleam (who must've been suffering from a slight loss of blood by now!) Suddenly the whole building became fab again and all the surrounding wastelands were transformed into sheer beauty (birds, bees, flowers, pretty girls, etc.). Galahad was given a magic island called Avalon for his trouble, but Lancelot and the other knights went back to Camelot.

Guinevere Again

Guinevere and Lancelot, although getting on a bit by now, couldn't keep apart (despite Lancelot's promise) and carried

*At least she got her dining-room table back. Ed

on their affair until eventually the black-hearted Mordred (son of Arthur and his half-sister, Morgause), split on them in open court. Arthur suddenly had to face the truth (this is a bit like *EastEnders*) and realized he'd have to burn his wife and cut his best mate Lancelot's head off.

But Lancelot escaped, killing three of his accusers on the way out, and leaving poor Guinevere to face the music (which doesn't seem very knightly behaviour to me). However, just as the poor old girl was about to go up in flames, six knights galloped up, cut her free, and charged off with her. One of them, of course, was Lancelot, and together they all dashed to the south coast and caught the first ferry to France.

Retribution

Arthur organized an expedition to get 'em back, and took half of his knights with him. They all ended up outside the Castle of the Joyous Guard at Benwick, France, where Lancelot was holed up with the dame and a small army. Lancelot knew he had to fight and sent a message out to Arthur asking him to forgive Guinevere and give her a safe passage home. Guinevere, being no fool (and a bit flaky), asked Arthur to come home with her and let Lancelot fight it out without him. But Arthur stayed put (quite right) and fought the battle – except he couldn't, because he found himself fighting against men that had once been his own noble knights and friends. He eventually got captured and was taken to Lancelot but, just as they were about to make it up, a young knight called Gawain, whose brothers had been killed when Lancelot escaped (are you with me?), challenged old Lance to a fight to the death. Lancelot, reluctantly, accepted.

It was a heck of a rumble, but Lancelot won at last and was pardoned by Arthur. Just as this happened, a bloke turned up from England with a message from the missus in London. It never rains but it pours. Guinevere said that Arthur's no-good son, Mordred, had claimed his dad had been killed and had made himself king. Worse still, he wanted to marry his dad's wife (Guinevere must have been a right old lady by now, I'd have thought). I thought going with your sister was bad enough, but your mother!!!*

So when Arthur got back to England a big war happened and our Arthur won hands down. But Mordred raised another, much bigger, army and this time the king looked as if he might lose. The old man really wanted to make a truce with Mordred and arranged to meet him the following day. Talk about bad luck: just as they were about to shake hands, a snake reared up and threatened to bite someone. Mordred drew his sword to kill it but when all his troops caught sight of the flashing blade they saw it as a sign to get stuck in.

Time's Up for Arthur
The battle raged for days until Camelot lay in ruins and

*She wasn't his mother – you haven't been paying attention. Ed

practically the only two soldiers left alive were Arthur and Mordred (funny that). Arthur promptly ran his son through with a spear but before Mordred bit the dust, the naughty lad caught his dad a fatal blow to the head. As the old king lay dying he told one of his few remaining knights to chuck Excalibur back into the lake. As he spoke, a white galleon with two beautiful women on board

turned up to save him. Some people have all the luck. One of them was Nyntve, the Lady of the Lake, and the other, believe it or not, was Morgan le Fay (remember?), his half-sister, who was now Queen of Avalon and really rather nice (so she changed, OK?). Arthur was carried aboard and off he went to Avalon, where he lived happily ever after. Presumably, at this point, Guinevere and Lancelot finally got it together (now in their nineties, no doubt) . . .

And now . . .
Back to real history . . .

Chapter 7

HERE COME THE VIKINGS!

Most people remember the Vikings best for their long, dragon-headed boats. Apart from being scary, one of their other great features was their flat bottoms (the boats, not the Vikings) – as this allowed them to sail up shallow rivers. This made invading a lot easier, as it meant they could ride in comfort right into the very heart of enemy country. You ask all the people who lived along the Seine, Rhine or Thames at that time.* It also meant that the Viking invaders could sail straight onto beaches, and avoid getting their socks wet.

America-on-Sea

Everyone likes to think that old Chris Columbus was the first explorer to dare to leave sight of land, and risk plunging off the edge of the world, but the Vikings had been doing it for donkey's years. From Iceland, they reached Greenland and a brave sailor called Bjarni Herjolfsson even spotted America when lost one day (later Leif Eriksson landed on it and called it Vinland). There is quite a lot of evidence that the Vikings even traded with China, mostly by meeting them half-way at Constantinople in Turkey.

*Tricky, I'd have thought. Ed

GOOSEBERRY WINE →

Useless Fact No. 614

Vinland means 'land of grapes', which is odd because they probably didn't have any – only cranberries and gooseberries, which they used to make wine.

. . . and Britain?

It all started up north. The Scandinavians had got wind of the collapse of the all-powerful Roman Empire and saw it as an opportunity to get their boats out again and check out what mischief they could get up to. They'd been having a hard time at home cos their bleak land couldn't support their growing population. By the ninth century the Scandinavian Vikings had set up home in many of the northern islands (only a day's sail away) putting them in a great position from which to launch all their murderous away-days in England. They then raided the north of Ireland and gradually moved down to Dublin – which unfortunately wasn't there yet.

In AD 793 a beastly bunch of boats bumped aground at Lindisfarne on the north-east coast of England and, after smashing the skulls of the kneeling monks and plundering the monastery, they went home to their wives and little Vikinglings. It was so incredibly easy (monks, as you can imagine, are pretty weedy fighters), that they decided to do it again the following summer, only this time with all their mates.

They soon became regular summer visitors (a bit like swallows*), raping and pillaging their way through the whole of the north-east of England, particularly Northumbria, where the Saxon farmers were a real pushover. Once, a vast fleet of

*Absolutely nothing like swallows. Ed

350 ships sailed up the Thames, stole a load of horses and rode around the Thames valley stealing or killing everything in sight. Cheeky, or what?

In no time at all the Vikings had a nice mini-empire consisting of Ireland, the Isle of Man and all of western England.

Viking Sagas

I know I said 'back to real history' before the start of this chapter, but one of the main problems with trying to find the truth about early Viking England is that you have to rely on 'sagas'. Like so much of early history, these sagas were a mixture of what really happened and a string of elaborate porkies designed to make the Vikings and their ancestors appear not only fab and brave, but kind as well. You know you're heading for trouble when you see the names of some of the writers and main characters: Eric Bloodaxe, Ragnor Hairy-Trousers, Harold Finehair, Ivar the Boneless – I could go on for ages (and pages).

° NAME THE VIKING °

We do know, however, that even the Vikings became fed up with raping and pillaging and continually living out of wooden boats (all those damp socks and pants). So much so, that soon after the first proper raids many of them decided to settle down and set up home here. As we know, there were kings a-plenty in England at this time and, despite them all being Christian, they still bickered and fought at every chance.

The situation couldn't have been better for anyone wanting to do a bit of light conquering. The Norwegian Vikings had their eyes on Cumberland and Lancashire, while the Danes took over eastern England and made Yorkshire a proper Danish kingdom.

Alfred for King!

But – hooray! – the mighty King Alfred of Wessex (and of burnt cakes fame) had other ideas. Alfred taught the native Saxons that although they didn't think much of towns they'd better start living in them, and fortifying them, if they wanted to protect themselves against these Viking raids. As a result, he stopped the Vikings getting any further into the south-west than Berkshire.

King Alfred eventually managed to show the Vikings the error of their ways, by not only making them tolerate Christianity but, more importantly, making them remain within the huge bit of land known as the Danelaw (which was basically everything between North Yorkshire and the River Thames). Everyone in this area had to speak Norse (of course). Alfred was therefore master of the whole of the South and West and defended it successfully against the dastardly Danish pirates.

But not for long . . .

This pact didn't last for ever and eventually the Danish Vikings were overrun by the Norwegian Vikings from the North. Meantime southern England finally gave in to a renewed attack from the Danes and, horror of horrors, the whole of England became part of the Danish Empire in 1016 under their King Canute (or Cnute, or Knut, or Kanute, or Kanoote, or . . . *). When he died, his useless sons frittered away all he had achieved and by 1066 England was good and ready to be invaded by Norman and his Williams – sorry, William and his Normans. But we're not there yet.

Vikings at Home

To be fair, the Danish and Norwegian Vikings who invaded us weren't any more civilized than the Saxons when it came to everyday living, and once they'd got over the initial difficulty (like – 'move over, we're coming to live in your space'), they got on rather well. The biggest problem was language, but as the Viking interlopers fancied the prettier Saxon girls (and even married 'em), it didn't take long to find a way of communicating. After all, you can't really be married to someone you can't talk to (or can you?*). Either way, the

*I thought you were in a hurry? Ed

mating of the two languages developed into an early form of the English we speak today.

Viking Farms

Much of the northern part of England was settled by Norse farmers who'd had enough of Ireland and were trying their luck here. They seemed to like it up north because the weather was much like they'd had back home: cold, dank and fairly miserable. They cleverly re-used stones from the remains of derelict farmhouses. The ones they rebuilt were long and low, thatched with a nice little hole in the middle of the roof to let the smoke out (and a door at the front to let the people in).

Everyone pitched in with the work on a Viking farm. As there were no schools, the kids were just another part of the work force (quite right too). Dad and the big brothers did all the heavy stuff, while mum and the nippers looked after, cooked and then served up the animals. They made all their own clothes from the yarn that they'd spun from the wool that they'd cut from the sheep that they'd reared. Neat, eh?

Town Time

Most Vikings were used to living in much larger groups back home, so all those that weren't particularly into farming would move into towns – or even set up their own. Anywhere that now ends in *-wick* (e.g. Berwick), *-ness* (Skegness), *-by* (Derby) or *-thorpe* (Scunthorpe) is usually of Viking origin.

At first they made buildings of wattle and daub (woven sticks plastered with mud) but later dug large pits with posts in the corners supporting low, thatched roofs. According to most

*That's another book, Mr Farman. Ed

historians, it was to cut down the draughts, which is pretty logical (if you don't mind living in a damp, smelly hole). Some even grew grass on their roofs . . . It's incredible to think that only a short time earlier, the amazing Romans had been knocking up truly magnificent and sophisticated buildings, even by today's standards, and had been used to living a life of considerable luxury. That's progress for you.

Up North

The Vikings captured York in 866 and, to the distress of the residents, made it the capital of northern England and called it Jorvik. It must have been confusing at first, because the people living there were all Christian and the Vikings still believed in all their own home-spun mumbo-jumbo.

York was crammed full of people (10,000 by 1066), so much so that the houses (2000 of 'em) had to be built sideways on to the streets to get them all in. (Why didn't they make the streets longer?) Lots is known about the way they lived, because York City Council, in its infinite wisdom, recently allowed a whole area called Coppergate to be dug up and studied. They found evidence of tanneries (for preparing leather), shoemakers, knife-makers, jewellers, blacksmiths and warehouses for storing the stuff brought up the river. The Vikings loved living in York, as it was a heck of a lot less harsh than what they'd been used to.

Lav Alert

The Vikings were very primitive indeed in the lavatorial department. Basically, they just dug a small lav-pit (with an optional plank across it) outside their house-pit. A few of these 'Vikolavs' were surrounded by wickerwork 'modesty screens' (which seems strange when you consider that they didn't turn a hair at doing much ruder things in public*).

NOT INVENTED YET. ED.

Viking Victuals (grub)

Anyone who's seen archaeologists at work or on telly will realize that they're often very weird people. Who else could get their kicks from examining lumps of fossilized human poo to discover what the Vikings ate? From the few prize specimens

*Do you *really* have to mention that? Ed

dug up at York, they reckon that the Vikings lived mostly on grain, but they also found the remains of corncockle seeds (which are poisonous and must have given them severe tummy aches if not chronic diarrhoea). They also found the tiny eggs of worms that must have come from the Vikings' stomachs. And these must originally have come from the microscopic wee beasties that lived in the dirty water from the lavs that no doubt leaked into their drinking water. Unfortunately, but understandably, in those days if they couldn't see something with the naked eye, it didn't exist. Simple, but rather dangerous when it comes to microscopic wee beasties that give you diarrhoea.

But you don't have to go to such lengths to discover what the Vikings and other people of that time ate. All sorts of pips, seeds and husks have been found, proving that they ate a wide range of fruit, nuts and vegetables like parsnips, cabbages, sprouts, carrots and the predecessor of the pea. They also kept cows and goats, so there's a fair chance they had a goodly supply of milk, butter, cheese and eggs.*

Useless Fact No. 615
The word 'steak' is connected to the word 'stick' because pieces of meat were cooked on sticks over fires. Fancy a nice juicy rump stick?

Viking Men-swear (or should that be Menswear?)
To your average peasant in the street, the Vikings didn't look a lot different to the people they were conquering, once you'd taken all those silly horned hats, fur jerkins and armour off. Having said that, so much of the poor blokes' time was spent

---

*Just a guess, but they probably would have had to keep chickens as well. Ed fighting, that they hardly ever got the chance to get out of their warrior-wear anyway. We do know, however, that Roman fashion (togas and all that fancy stuff) was long forgotten by the eighth century and fashion continued in pretty much the same vein as it had before they came along.

Where are They Now?

Although you don't see that many Vikings in your local supermarket, you do occasionally see people who look as if they might once have been (Vikings): tall, with rugged features, thick blond hair and – oh yes – helmets with horns on. Seriously though, those early Scandinavians did have quite an influence on the way we Brits look today.

Chapter 8

THE END
(AND THE BEGINNING)

Alfred popped his clogs in the year 899, leaving England quite peaceful (ish). This peace was ruined by a certain Ethelred the Unready (don't ask, it's a long story and this is a short book), an Anglo-Saxon king who had a habit of killing all the Danes he could get his hands on, particularly those living in York. This annoyed the Danish Vikings no end, and to show it, they invaded again in 1016, led by Sven Forkbeard, so called because of his beard (which was forked).* It was his son Kanoote (is that right?) who not only became King of England and the whole of the Scandinavian Empire but married Ethelred's widow as well. Smart lad!

During King Canute's 20-year rule the English and the Danes and the Norsemen moved much closer together. The Vikings let their own beliefs go and started building Christian-style churches, even speaking *English* English instead of Viking English. We do still use lot of Viking words, however (*awkward, odd, sly, weak, guess* and *glitter* for instance) and in the Orkneys they still use *driv, fug, murr, hagger* or *dug* to describe all the different kinds of rain. I just say *wet* – how's about you?

Like all good empires, this one collapsed and Ethelred's son, Edward the Confessor, got his old man's country back in 1041. Edward turned out to be a bit of a wimp and the job of

*You don't say. Ed

ruling was actually done by a chap called Harold of Wessex. Harold simply hated those pesky Normans who were beginning to look a little threatening, across the water in Normandy. These Normans, who'd once been Vikings (as you'd know by now if you'd been concentrating), had had their eyes on Britain for ages, but were looking for the right opportunity, and the right guy, to lead them into an invasion . . .

Lighting-up Time

When head-Norman William heard about Harold's aversion to Normans, he was well miffed and, without further ado, decided to invade England and become its king – which he did . . . and did.

Everyone knows about 1066, good old William the Conqueror, the Battle of Hastings, arrows in eyes and all that, so I won't bother with it now. Save to say that as soon as the Normans took over our fair land, things started cheering up and the lights came on, not only in England, but all over Europe. The Dark Ages were officially over, thank goodness.

☞ TIME'S UP

I don't know about you, but I reckon that living in the Dark Ages wasn't up to much, unless you were a king or a knight or a princess or something. Having said that, I expect most of my male readers would have quite liked life as a Viking – all that pillaging and feasting and not washing, etc.

Anyway, I hope you now know a bit more about the Dark Ages than you did before, but if you don't, you can't really complain. After all, what do you expect for £1.99 – the *Encyclopedia Britannica*? If you want to know more, there's always the local or school library. However, if, like me, you're in a hurry, then avoid them and go to your local bookshop and try another in the series. If you walk slowly I should have written another couple by the time you get there.